Self-Discipline

21 Days to Develop Your Confidence, Willpower and Motivation

Table of Contents

Introduction

I want to thank you and congratulate you for purchasing the book, "Self-Discipline: 21 Days to Develop Your Confidence, Willpower, and Motivation."

This book contains proven steps and strategies on how to develop self-discipline and alter your will power to attain more in life. Motivation and willpower are two of the toughest qualities for a human being to develop, owing to a natural tendency of succumbing to self-doubt and restraint. But it is critical to develop a high level of self-respect and remain as motivated as possible, to attain all the best things in life.

If you are one such person looking to enhance your motivation by increasing your self-discipline, then you have come to the right place. In this book, we will explore the meaning of motivation, willpower and self-discipline and how you can use all three to your advantage.

It can be utilized as a guide to change your attitude towards life and take things a little more seriously to attain more from it. You can work towards fulfilling your distant goals and ambitions without having to forgo living your life. You will see that 21 days are all that you need to change yourself and develop a certain confidence required to enhance your overall living.

Thanks again for purchasing this book, I hope you enjoy it!

Chapter 1: Confidence, Willpower, and Motivation

We often hear these words, Confidence, Willpower and Motivation; but do you understand what these words stand for? In this first chapter, we will look at the difference between confidence, motivation, and willpower in detail to have a better understanding of these concepts.

What is motivation?

Motivation is a very broad subject that can be interpreted in many different ways. For a layman, the best way to interpret it is by understanding what a "motive" stands for. As it is commonly known, a motive refers to an impulse that guides a person's actions. If the desire is not strong enough, then the person will not bother to respond to it. It will only work if the motivating factor is high enough to elicit a response from the individual. This stimulus can vary on a daily basis and can depend on a person's surroundings.

There can be many things in life that can help a person remain motivated. After all, it is quite important to go after one's dreams and ambitions to make the most of life. However, it is easier said than done. A person is required to have a high sense of motivation to achieve whatever he sets his mind on.

As mentioned earlier, the stimulus should be strong enough for a person to be motivated enough to take action. In this day and age with cutthroat competition on the rise, the idea of being motivated to achieve one's deep desires is almost nonexistent. It boils down to competing with others while having to forgo one's dreams and ambitions.

This leads to conditions such as stress and anxiety as the person will not be able to chase after his goals and ambitions and remain caught up in a web of competition. Again, that is not the only place where motivation falls short, as people tend to forgo their dreams in search of material possessions. Although that also can lead to motivation, it may not last long. If you wish to understand motivation on a scientific basis, then you can go through the different theories, which will explain the different kinds of motivation.

Intrinsic motivation

Intrinsic motivation refers to the one who is inborn. A person can be motivated from within to go after his dreams and desires. A person will remain internally driven without the help of an outside source. This type of motivation is quite hard to generate, as it is not easy to feel internally motivated. The person has to be quite passionate and set himself/herself high-level goals and pursue them to remain motivated.

Extrinsic motivation

Extrinsic motivation, on the other hand, refers to being motivated by outside sources. These can be from the surroundings, people, and events that motivate people to attain the best in life. Extrinsic motivation can come from many different places and is not subject to any fixed source. It also greatly depends on the person's perception of motivation and how he or she interprets it.

Combination

A person can have a combination of both intrinsic and extrinsic motivation. He or she can be motivated by their surroundings as well as their internal feelings. In fact, it is best to have a combination as compared to just any one of these as he or she will be better able to attain their goals and desires.

If you want to exercise self-control, then you have to develop a strong sense of motivation. You have to understand the basic requirement to remain motivated and keep it in loop.

What is confidence?

Confidence comes from the Latin word confidere, which means 'to be sure.' As you know, a confident person is someone who is sure of something that he is doing. He or she is aware of his or her full potential and operates out of surety. This type of confidence helps a person achieve more out of life. A confident person is someone who does not indulge in self-doubt. He or she is well aware of his or her capabilities and moves forward confidently.

Self-confidence refers to having full faith in oneself and knowing that you will do the right thing. This type of confidence is quite important to develop especially if you want to attain the best in life.

Let us look at two examples to understand the concept better. Say two friends are trying out for a spot on their school basketball team. Both of them are equally skilled and can both be selected based on their efforts. However, one is quite confident whereas the other is not so much. The confident child will be able to perform better as he or she will not be under any pressure. He will be quite confident in his abilities and put in a worthy effort. On the other hand, the child who lacks confidence will put up an effort that is marred by under confidence and pressure to excel. The two will not allow him to put in a worthy effort.

This shows that regardless of whether or not you have the talent to achieve something in life, you will have to approach it confidently. It is your confidence that will help you succeed in life. However, that does not mean you can be extremely confident and attain whatever you wish to without putting in the required effort. You have to have the talent and mix it with confidence to accomplish the best out of life.

General confidence

General confidence refers to having an inborn confidence. The person need not be influenced by an outside source to develop this type of confidence. He or she will be internally motivated to put on their best performance and attain the best in life.

Specific confidence

Specific confidence is seen as a precursor to general confidence. A person who is internally motivated will have a good sense of specific confidence. He or she will lay the foundation for general confidence and attain life's goals. Focused confidence is a good way to enhance one's self-esteem.

Between the two, it is more important for a person to have general confidence as it considered as a constant factor that is required to enhance and boost motivation. Even if a person is extremely confident in specific areas, he or she may not be able to attain all that they desire. The only way to have it is by having a strong sense of general confidence.

Over-confidence

It is quite important not to be overconfident. Overconfidence is a situation where a person possesses too much confidence. He or she will not be able to tell between basic confidence and over confidence and end up doing too much. This will start to become an obstruction and prevent the person from reaching their goals. However, overconfidence is a quality that is mostly inherent, and the most important thing is for a person to stave it off as much as possible. Ego is what mostly drives overconfidence and dictates a situation. The person will not be able to control it and end up giving into his or her whims. The only way of doing so is by remaining alert and making sure that the ego is not taking over. A seasoned person will be able to successfully keep his overconfidence at bay and not allow it to interfere in his life.

What is willpower?

Willpower is the next quality that you should develop. As you know, it is quite important to have all those qualities that will help you attain all that you desire in life. You have to be able to combine them together to make it easier for you to pursue your goals and ambitions.

Willpower, again, is entirely subjective and differs from person to person. Some people can have a strong sense of will-power while others might have it quite low.

Will power mainly depends on how a person perceives their surroundings and uses it to enhance his or her life. For example, a person can be influenced by an external source and have their will power affected by it. It may rise up or go down depending on the person's perception of things.

In general terms, will power is mostly determined by a person's need to excel. If he or she is motivated enough and garners good self-control then will find it easy to develop a strong will power.

Here is looking at some of the qualities that a person with strong will power needs to develop

- The ability to understand the difference between short and long term goals and be able to pursue them
- The ability to override unnecessary temptations and remain on the right path
- The ability to not give into temptations and remain calm through any situation
- The ability to consciously regulate oneself

These are some of the qualities of strong will power. This varies from person to person.

It is quite easy to enhance willpower through determination and hard work. A person can increase his will power by putting his mind to it. Through the course of this book, we will look at how you can influence your will power and increase it.

As you can see, there is an apparent difference between all three. But it is quite important for you to possess a combination of all three in order to attain the best out of life.

Chapter 2: Activities for Day One to Three

When it comes to increasing motivation and self-control, you have to remain patient and allow your mind to adapt to the new changes. If you rush into things, then you will not be able to see lasting results and therefore must come up with a plan that will slowly introduce these changes in your life.

It is believed that it takes 21 days for a person to develop a new habit. This is the time that the brain takes to understand a habit and allow it to become a part of everyday life. In this chapter, we will look at the things that you can do on the first 11 days of your journey, to foster a permanent change.

Day 1
Identifying the situation

The very first step of the process will be to identify where you currently stand. This refers to knowing what your current situation is, by analyzing your motivation, self-control and confidence levels.

It is understood that all human beings are born with all three of these qualities, and it is inherent for people to feel confident, motivated and exercise self-control. It is vital for you to know where yours lie as then you can alter it and raise it up.

You can start by making a note of your everyday activities. Maintain a book and write down everything that you do for a week. Right from the time you get up till you go to bed, make a list of all the activities that you do on a daily basis. You have to record the events in chronological order and write down what it is and why you are performing it. It will pay to divide the book into mundane/routine housework and office work as you can easily refer to it at a later date.

The basic idea is to look at the tasks that come your way and how motivated/confident you are while performing them. You can assign a task a level such as level 1 being toughest and level 10 being the easiest and see how you fare. If you are highly motivated and confident then you can reward yourself a point between 1 and 5, if you are not as motivated or confident in performing the task, then you can assign between 5 and 10.

At the same time, you must also ask a family member and a friend or colleague to write down what they observe. Doing so will help you compare your thoughts with that of another person so that you can match the two.

Once you have finished with the two, you can compare your scores and see how motivated you think you are and how others have perceived it.

Day 2
Removing the obstacles

Next, you have to make a separate list of the obstacles that stand in your way. This is to see what is stopping you from going after your goals and ambitions. With the prepared list, you will be able to see what is causing you to feel demotivated or lack confidence. It can range from personal issues to distractions, and you must make a list of them.

As you know, it is quite necessary for you to remove these obstacles if you wish to enhance your confidence and motivation. It might seem like a tough task but is important for you to deal with them as soon as possible so that you can increase your confidence and motivation. The obstacles might seem a little overwhelming but is important for you to deal with them as efficiently as you can. You have to write them down so that you know what you are dealing with and deal with them one after the other.

These obstacles can be both mental and physical in nature and will be important for you to address them separately. You have to come up with a plan to escape them so that you can remain on the right track. As mentioned earlier, you should allow it sufficient time so that your mind and body can adjust to it. After the first week of observation, you have to spend a day in analyzing and coming with solutions to the problems.

You should put in the right effort to fulfill this task. You can write them down along with the solutions to start working on them as soon as possible. For example, if you are unable to finish a task at the office then you must look at what is holding you back from doing so. If it is a distraction, then you must work on dealing with it and reducing it down to size.

Day 3
Making a plan

The next step is to create a plan to develop confidence and motivation. Once you have successfully identified the problems and come up with solutions to deal with them, you have to make a plan to tackle them one after another.

You can complete this task on the 11th day so that you can start working on it by the 12th. The plan should be a little flexible so that you can do more if you can fit it in. Having a very rigid plan might also help you stick better with it.

You can work with a friend or relative to come up with the plan that you can follow. You can also use another plan as a reference point to come up with one of your own.

The plan should be easy enough to be implemented within the next ten days. You have to ensure that you put in 100% effort towards it so that you avail lasting results.

These are the different steps that you must implement in the first 3 days. Again, it is best for you to make a plan that is easy to implement. You need not stick to this routine alone and use it as a blueprint to come up with one of your own.

Chapter 3: Day Four to Six

The next ten days will be for you to implement the plan that you have made. As you know, making a plan is always just the beginning and is important for you to take appropriate action.

Here is looking at the steps that you can implement to get started with it.

Day 4
Implementing the plan

The first step on day 4 is for you to apply the solutions that you came up to solve the existing and impending issues. It is easier said than done, as you have to put in the required effort. You need to ensure that you have what it takes to not only put the plan to practice but also be able to make the changes stick.

You have to make a conscious effort towards implementing them and make sure that you pay 100% attention to it. It is a good idea to remain as attentive during the process as possible so that you can remain with the results for longer. Say for example you have identified the problem as being a physical one. You are not physically motivated to do a task because you don't find the result to be appealing enough. In such a case, you have to start by changing your mindset. You should tell yourself that the result should not be the primary focus of taking up the task and it is the effort that will ultimately count.

As you know, it is quite tough to convince yourself mentally than it is to physically. You will be able to take action only if you put your mind to it and are fully capable of undertaking the action. You must also make up your mind to enjoy the process. As mentioned earlier, your mind should be in a position to put your body to the task. If you remain mentally disinterested in something, then it will be quite difficult for you to fulfill the task.

Don't think of it as a task and consider it to be more of any activity. Think of it as a means to enhance your overall living and to be able to do more with your life. Again, it helps to have the company of someone who can inspire you to put in your best efforts. Inspiration will help you remain on track and do more in less time. The inspiration can be a role model. You can emulate their moves to attain success.

You will have to do this for the next ten days and make sure that you stick to the plan. You can stick hard copies of it so that you are reminded of what you should be doing. It will be a good idea for you to also maintain a soft copy of the plan so that you can refer to it from time to time.

Remember that only you are responsible for your progress and must put in the effort to attain what you desire. When it comes to enhancing your personal motivation, you have to ensure that you work towards it by prioritizing it and ensuring that you are 100% focused on the task at hand.

No task should be considered menial, and everything should be viewed as an important task.

Day 5
Measuring progress

You have to measure your progress. It is important for you to check your progress to ensure that you are on the right track.

The best way to do so is by performing the first task all over again. You can start by recording your activities once again and check your progress. You can use the same activity list as you did before, as it will be easier for you to measure your progress. You can write down how motivated you are now and how much more effort you are putting in towards completing a task.

You must also check whether you finish the task thoroughly before moving on to another one. This is an important aspect that you must pay attention to. If you leave a task half way, then it will be quite useless even if you put in 100% effort at the beginning. It will only mean that you lost interest and were not motivated enough to complete the task.

You can also assign the task to the same family member and colleague as before to observe you and the effort you are putting into fulfilling the tasks. Once it is done, you can then compare the two and see where you stand. You will see a difference in your markings, as your mind will constantly tell you to perform something in a better manner. But you have to aim towards attaining a vast difference in your motivation and confidence levels so that you can call it a success.

Day 6
Follow-up

You have to follow up with the plans. You would have completed a week with the program and time for you to look back at the journey you have had thus far.

Remember that the habit building will occur over a 21-day period and should be followed up after that time. You cannot leave it at that as you might lapse into your old habits.

You have to make sure that you work towards remaining motivated for life. Those that do not follow it up will not be able to maintain their newfound habit. As is understood, it takes 21 days to form a habit and will take around the same to break it. It is, therefore, important not to lapse into old habits and give the new ones a chance to stay.

Make sure you check your progress every week. You will have to continue with the process of making plans and implementing them. Only then will you able to make the habits stay.

These form the different steps that you can take on day 4 to 6. Again, you can use this as a blueprint and come up with one of your own.

Chapter 4: Day Seven to Twenty

When you are in pursuit of developing confidence, motivation and strengthening your will power, it is quite important for you to follow certain daily rituals that will help you remain focused.

Once the first week is up, you can take up the following daily rituals. It is best for you to do these one-day at a time so that you have the chance to develop a habit.

Here is looking at daily habits that you can adopt to remain focused.

Day 7
Meditation

Meditation is one of the most important habits to develop when you are in pursuit of motivation and confidence. Meditation helps you relieve stress and put your mind to good use. You can easily tap into your subconscious and pull out qualities that will help you remain on course. You can try out many types of meditation such as chanting meditation and walking meditation. To perform the previous type, start by finding yourself a quiet corner and assume the lotus position. Now draw in deep breaths and close your eyes. Focus on inhaling and exhaling at a rapid pace and clearing out your thoughts with every exhalation. Do this for 15 to 20 minutes on a daily basis to experience mental bliss. If you don't have the patience to sit in one place and meditate then you can try out walking meditation. To perform this type of meditation, you can pick a starting point and start walking regularly. When you place your right leg forward, you must draw in a deep breath and exhale while placing your left foot forward.

Continue doing so until you feel light. You can perform both types of meditation on a daily basis to get rid of stress and remain blissful.

Day 8
Physical activity

If you wish to remain mentally alert, then it is quintessential for you to exercise on a regular basis. Exercising helps in reducing stress and promotes the release of serotonin. It is a chemical that helps in curbing stress and enhances mental well being. Exercising also helps in improving concentration to a large extent. If you are easily distracted and unable to exercise control over your will power, then you can depend on exercising to help you out. You can take up a routine that helps you avail at least an hour of cardio exercise. You can hit the gym if you are not motivated enough to exercise by yourself. You can also take up a sport such as basketball or swimming to remain physically active. Dancing is also a great way to stay fit and mentally alert. As per studies, those that suffer from addictions such as alcoholism and smoking were better able to cope with withdrawing from these activities, just by exercising on a regular basis.

Day 9
Meals

Make sure that you consume power meals that will keep your mind alert and active. Foods have the capacity to help your mind remain active and help you make important decisions. If you consume junk and processed foods, then they can alter your thinking by increasing the level of cortisol in your brain. Cortisol has the power to interfere with your thinking and make it tough for you to make important decisions. It can also hamper your productivity and make it difficult for you to finish a task. You can consume those foods that are rich in omega 3 fatty acids as they can enhance your mental capacity. Some of them include freshwater fish and flax seeds. You must also consume fresh fruits and vegetables as they can reduce oxidative damage and make you more alert. You can prepare a meal plan that will help you get started with it. You can also keep all the ingredients ready so that it will be easier for you to prepare the meals.

Day 10
Bad habits

It is quite necessary to put an end to bad habits, especially if you want to be a bit more productive. Bad habits such as drinking and smoking can interfere with your life's goals and how you pursue them. They don't only affect you physically but also mentally. You will see that your productivity has decreased and are unable to do your tasks on time. You should take care of your body as much as you can to develop confidence, motivation and enhance self-control. You can practice yoga and meditation to reduce the effects of the bad habit and also increase your mental capacity.

Day 11
Be accountable

It is known that most of us are extremely busy in life doing one thing or another and prefer to procrastinate as much as we can. But this will only lead to a delay in our achievements thereby making it quite important not to procrastinate and do everything on time. One good way of being alert is by being more accountable. You have to take more responsibility and do more in less time. If you have made a promise to someone, then it is important for you to keep up with the same. You should not procrastinate keeping up with the promise and try to achieve whatever you have set out to. A good way to keep your promise and be more accountable is by having a partner to share it with. You can choose whoever you like and match your schedule with theirs. That way, you can always check each other's progress and ensure that the two of you are on the right track. Make sure that you don't make excuses to each other and complete your tasks on time.

Day 12
End goals

It is a good idea for you to make a list of goals on a daily basis. It is understood that everybody is extremely busy and has no time to indulge in small tasks. But a good way of remaining alert and staving off procrastination is by making lists. You can make a list of things that you wish to finish by the end of the day. The list can be exhaustive and make sure you leave a space at the bottom to write down as you go. A list like that can act as a physical reminder of the things that you need to do within the course of the day and help you remain on top of your schedule. You can use a cell phone app to help you make a list and carry it around with you through the day to look at the list. With time, you will see that the list has made you more productive and can do more in a day than before. But make sure you don't recycle the list and do different tasks on a daily basis.

Day 13
Affirmations

It is quite necessary for you to recite positive affirmations. Positive affirmations will help you enhance your mental well being and put you on the course. These affirmations can be your own or can also be borrowed from famous quotes. The point is to allow them to help you improve your motivational level. You can also look up to a role model to help you increase your confidence. Reading up on a famous autobiography can also help you stay on course. It can be something you have already read and inspired you in the past. You can download a few inspirational quotes on your phone and read them in the mornings. This will make sure that you will be in a place to keep yourself motivated throughout the day and complete all your tasks. Some positive affirmations include "I will remain motivated every day," "I am full of confidence," "I will put my best efforts in everything I do" etc. These will help you remain on track and help you enhance your confidence levels on a daily basis.

Day 14
Partner up

It is always a good idea to partner up. You and your partner can always keep each other motivated. The partner can be anyone including a friend and a spouse. The two of you can always keep track of each other's activities and make sure that you are on the right track. You need not share the same goals and ambitions but can always keep track of it. A motivational talk with a loved one in the morning can go a long way in keeping you motivated throughout the day.

Day 15
Profess

It is a good idea for you to profess about your goals and ambitions. It will help you stay on course with it and ensure that you take it seriously. You can write a blog so that you can speak about your motivations. You can also join a group where you get to meet other people who are motivational and confident. You can talk to them about your ambitions and remain on course. You can also get them to check your progress as well. If no such group meets up in your area, then you can consider starting one by yourself. You can announce about it on your social media site and get people to join in.

Day 16
Distractions

One of the biggest issues that most people face these days is distraction. A person can get easily distracted by the many things around him and is important to keep them at bay. One good way of doing so is by identifying these distractions and cutting down on them as much as possible. You have to make a list of all those things that are distracting you and see to it that you do not indulge in them when you are doing something important. These can include checking your phone, indulging in social media, listening to music, etc. If these are your distractions, then you must avoid indulging them during your productive hours. You can assign them their individual times like watching TV at night and listening to music before going to bed and not let them interfere with your daily activity. You can enhance your productivity by remaining focused on the task without being distracted easily. Once the task is done, you can relax by indulging in the activity. Try not to cut it off completely as you will not be able to focus on your work.

Day 17
Prioritize

It is a golden rule to prioritize your life's goals so that you can get more out of your time. Prioritizing refers to making a list of all the things you want to achieve and going about them in an orderly fashion. You have to place the important tasks on top to ensure that they get done first and then go after the other ones. As you know, prioritizing is important in all fields of life and more so with everyday tasks. With time, you will see that it is possible for you to do more in less time and also finish all your tasks before hand. You need not follow this rule for your daily tasks alone and also use it for your long term plans. You can place the tasks in order and tick them off one by one. It also pays to set a timeline for your tasks so that you can finish them on time before moving on to the next.

Day 18
Productivity first

Leave all your productive tasks for the morning. Many people start with useless tasks in the morning so as to get done with them as soon as possible and then move on to important ones. But this is the wrong way of going about it, as you have first to tackle the important tasks and then move on to the smaller ones. You will be quite fresh and alert in the morning and capable of finishing off a task better. You have to stick with this plan so as to ensure that you complete the toughest tasks in the best possible way. When you make your morning list, make sure that you place the important tasks at the top and the unimportant ones at the bottom and go about it in that order. If a strategy is working well for you, then you should stick with it and ensure that you follow the same on a daily basis. Similarly, if some routine has not worked well for you in the past, then it is best to take a lesson from it and not repeat it again.

Day 19
Delegate

Do not refrain from delegating an activity to another person, as it will help you be more productive and exercise more control over your tasks. Delegating can seem like a tough task especially if you wish to have more control over it. However, doing so can help you to a large extent and allow you to get done faster. You can make a list of the tasks and the people who you wish to delegate the task to and assign it one by one. You must overlook it from time to time to ensure that they are doing their task on time. It is quite important for you first to identify the person's capacity before handing out the task as otherwise; it might eat away into your time and productivity. You can appoint someone to supervise for you, so you can remain focused on your own task and not worry about the delegated work. You can always announce a reward for whoever does the best job as that way they will make an additional effort towards doing the work in a better manner.

Day 20
Nighttime habit

It is a good idea for you to develop a nighttime habit that will help you calm down. This can be taking a shower before hitting the bed or maintaining a journal. Doing so will help you wake up feeling refreshed. You can consider getting your partner involved as well so that the two of you can enjoy the benefits. Make sure that you keep up with the ritual and not end it too soon.

These form the different daily activities that you can take up when you wish to enhance your self-control and strengthen your confidence. But you need not limit yourself to just these and do other things that can help you stay on course.

Chapter 5: Day 21 - Chakra Balancing

Here is what you can do on the 21st day. This will be the last day of your journey and must make the most of it.

When it comes to increasing your motivation, confidence, and self-control, you have to work on the many different aspects that govern it. It is not limited to developing new habits and maintaining them and also involves maintaining a healthy body.

The body consists of 7 imaginary wheels known as chakras that are vertically placed at equal distances in the center of the body. Each chakra is connected to a set of organs and helps in keeping the body functioning well. These chakras rotate at a certain speed and maintain good organ health. Each one ultimately helps in keeping the mind alert and a person motivated.

Here is looking at the placement of the different chakras in the body.

The first chakra lies behind the pubic bone and governs a person's self- confidence. If there is a blockage here, then the person will indulge in self-doubt and not be able to carry out daily activities. The person might also suffer from ego issues and not be able to lead a normal life.

The second chakra is placed below the navel and deals with a person's confidence. Those that have a blockage here might feel less confident and not be able to fulfill a task with ease.

The third chakra lies below the sternum and signifies a person's self-control and power. If there is a blockage here, then he or she will not be able to operate confidently and will be held back to a large extent.

The fourth chakra is the heart chakra and deals with a person's self-love. Those that have a blockage here will not love themselves and engage in self-doubt. This can lead to demotivation and a lack of confidence.

The fifth chakra lies in the center of the throat and deals with a person's communication. This can be both external and internal communication. Some people might not be able to understand their feelings and get tangled up in a web of feelings that are not communicated.

The sixth chakra lies in between the eyebrows and deals with a person's intuition. It guides a person's sixth sense. A blockage her can mean an inability to sense things that are not perceived.

The seventh chakra lies inside the mind of a person. It guides his or her motivation and confidence. It also signifies intelligence, which is indirectly related to motivation and confidence. A blockage here can mean the person is unable to remain motivated and confident.

There are many ways in which the blockages can be removed. Here is looking at some of the ways.

Crystal healing

You can make use of crystals to improve your chakra health. These crystals are said to possess certain powers that help in cleaning the chakras. Each one has a particular stone that can be used to cleanse the chakra. For example, the first chakra can be cleansed using a red calcite. You can place it above the area corresponding to the chakra and cover it with a pyramid to trap and circulate the energy within it. This will ensure that the negative energy is removed and a positive one is introduced. Similarly, you can work on all the other chakras and cleanse them one by one. You can carry the activity once or twice a week to keep your chakras clean and healthy.

Meditation

You can perform kundalini meditation to cleanse your chakras. Kundalini meditation refers to cleansing your chakras thoroughly. You can assume the lotus position and close your eyes. Now imagine a ball of light as originating in your first chakra and cleansing it thoroughly. It then moves to the second, then third, then fourth, fifth, sixth and finally the seventh before ultimately leaving your body. Another light then originates and so on and so forth. You have to imagine this for the next 10 to 12 minutes. An alternative is to practice Qi Gong meditation. Here, instead of imagining the ball of light, you will instead imagine a ball of water as moving between the first, fourth and seventh chakra. This will leave you feeling thoroughly refreshed. You can perform this once or twice a week. You can combine it with your regular meditational routine to feel thoroughly enriched.

Aura cleansing

The aura is an imaginary film that surrounds a person. It consists of many different colors, and each one is connected to a particular chakra. For example, the first chakra will form a red film around the body and the second will form a yellow ring. A person can have their aura read to know which chakra is blocked. A professional aura reader will be able to tell you just by looking at your aura. If a particular color is dull or has holes in it, then it means that the chakra attached to it needs to be healed and cleansed.

One good way of cleansing the aura is by standing in sunlight. Aura tends to expand and can heal to a large extent. You can play a sport under the sun to help you experience a difference. This expansion of the aura will automatically increase your confidence levels and enhance your personality. You will start feeling quite enriched and dynamic.

You can also use some sea salt to rub over yourself or take a cold shower. Both of these will help you cleanse your aura as also your chakras.

These are the different things that you can do to cleanse your aura and enhance your overall personality.

Remember that this is part of alternate science and up to your interpretation. There is no scientific evidence available for the same.

Chapter 6: Key Highlights

Motivation is one of the most important virtues to possess in life. Those that do not feel motivated will not be able to achieve what they set out to attain in their lifetime. Motivation is determined by a person's need to excel and can be regarded as a natural stimulant. Motivation and confidence go hand in hand and are both important for a person to possess.

It is true that everybody is born with a certain level of motivation. But as time passes by, people tend to get busy and forgo remaining motivated. This can negatively impact their lives, as they will not be able to chase after their dreams.

It is possible for a person to increase his level of confidence and motivation just by following a few everyday steps. The person can enhance his way of thinking and acquire more in life. Motivation and confidence are both easy to alter if the person remains determined about it.

It takes just 21 days for a person to develop a new habit and you too can improve motivation and confidence in the same time frame. All that it will take is a little determination and the will to change for good. Once you remain determined, you will have the chance to change yourself for the better.

You might resist it a little at the beginning but will be able to settle into it with time. The main aim will be to increase one's motivational level in life. It can help in enhancing a person's overall persona to a large extent. He or she will be more determined in life to go after their dreams and ambitions.

Self-control is the third most important component that a person should possess. Those that are unable to exercise self-control will not be able to move ahead in life and get caught up in tangles. It is, therefore, important to exercise as much control as possible to enhance your ambitions.

You can follow three simple steps in the first ten days of the program starting with analyzing your current position. This will tell you exactly where you stand regarding your motivational level and what you can do to further influence it. Next, you can make a list of the tasks that you perform and how motivated you feel to fulfill them. It is quite important to figure out what is holding you back and fix the issue. But before doing so, you have to come up with a plan that will allow you to repair the issues for good.

Next, you have to implement the plans to start building your confidence and motivation. This can take around ten days to implement and take off. You have to remain patient and ensure that you take the right steps towards it. After 21 days are up, you must check where you lie and measure your progress. This is an important step, as you must know how much you have progressed. Based on it, you can follow up with the same routine.

Remember, it is quite important to keep up with the habit as you might forget about it in the next 21 days. That is exactly how long it takes to undo a habit and so, will be quite important for you to keep up with it.

There are some daily habits that you must develop that will further enhance your chances of increasing your motivation and confidence. These habits should be part of your everyday life and not limited to 21 days alone. This includes taking care of your body by exercising and consuming fresh, nutritious food. Increasing your mental strength by meditating and finding a partner to join you in your endeavors. You must also write down and recite positive affirmations that can help you improve your mental capacity.

Chakra healing is an alternate science that can be used to enhance confidence and motivation. You can take it up before or after the 21 days. The main objective is to create a situation where your chakras are thoroughly cleansed and prepared to help you increase your motivation and confidence. Once you take up the activities you will see that it is possible for you to remain more determined to go after the different goals and ambitions in life and improve your self-control.

Conclusion

I want to thank you again for purchasing this book!

I hope this book was able to help you to understand why it is important for you to develop confidence, motivation and self-discipline. Though these words are casually thrown around when people talk everyday, each of these have a deep impact and meaning in our lives.

To find success, you have to be able to mold and shape them to your liking. All it will take is 21 days for you to alter your life and achieve everything that you set out to achieve. The changes mentioned in this book are not big but the impact they will have on your life will change the way you perceive life.

The next step is to put into practice all the advice mentioned in this book so that you can experience the desired outcome. So what are you waiting for? Go on and apply these changes and at the end of 21 days you will discover a new and improved you.

All the best!

Finally, if you enjoyed this book, then I'd like to ask you for a favor, would you be kind enough to leave a review for this book on Amazon? It'd be greatly appreciated!

Thank you and good luck!

Preview Of 'Yoga: 4-Week Step By Step Guide for Yoga Beginners'

Introduction

We live in a world where we feel completely lost and just riding along. We feel as if we just exist without any particular purpose in life. When that happens, anxiousness, stress and depression starts creeping in, and we stop taking care of how we look as well as our health. The result is an unhealthy lifestyle, which may even advance to various health complications. Have you gotten to that point of your life where you feel you need to find your purpose and bring order to your currently disorderly life?

Well, yoga can do all that since it can help you to bring the much needed order in your physical, mental and spiritual life. What do you think yoga is? Do you think of it as simply executing Olympics level gymnastics stunts? Well, yoga is much more than these stunts. This book will introduce you to yoga, what it is all about and how you can start practicing yoga in as little as 4 weeks.

The Basics

"*Yoga*" is a Sanskrit word formed from a Latin word '*yoke*' meaning to join. From a human perspective, the easiest way to understand yoga is to view it as a union of various aspects of the human spirit and body such as the physical, mental, and spiritual being.

In simpler language, we can define yoga as spiritual techniques and exercises that are designed to 'join' your body and mind. It also can help you attain oneness with the universe. Yoga also helps you achieve a healthier lifestyle because it facilitates weight loss, improves blood circulation, and boosts your flexibility.

As we shall see later in the book, different yoga techniques and Asanas demand for specific approaches to derive the expected benefits: unification of various aspects of the human spirit.

In this guide, we shall look at yoga from a varied perspective in a bid to help you derive the benefits offered by yoga.

Before we start discussing how to practice yoga, let us look at the benefits you stand to gain by practicing yoga. By looking at these benefits, you will feel inspired to start your 4-week Yoga challenge.

Why Practice Yoga?

Yoga uses various spiritual and physical exercises that bring many benefits to yoga yogis and yoginis (these are the respective names given to male and female yoga practitioners). For instance, yoga is useful for weight loss, building muscles, relieving stress, and strengthening the heart.

Regular practice can also help you achieve inner peace especially if you pair yoga with meditation. If you are looking for a refreshing leisure activity, yoga can still be an interesting exercise you can practice alone or with friends. Whatever reason you may have for wanting to become a yogi or yogini, yoga can deeply connect your mind, body, and spirit, which can help you experience your real self.

Let us detailedly discuss the various benefits yoga has for its practitioners:

1. Boosts Physical Fitness

Yoga uses various poses and stretches; what we call asanas. Research shows that holding asanas for at least 60 seconds can boost your posture and deadlift strength. Yoga can boost balance of strength onto your opposing muscle groups, and help you improve flexibility and range of motion.

The good thing is that yoga poses are simple and can fit everyone ranging from body builders, athletes, the obese, and members of either gender. When practiced properly, yoga reduces stress buildup in the muscles, relaxes you, and prevents possible workout injuries because it improves flexibility.

To benefit from yoga in terms of strength gains, elongated muscles, and boosting physical fitness, its best to adopt yoga as part of your regular workout program. For instance, doing yoga stretches before strength training allows the muscles to freely workout without actually shutting down in response to stretched tendons.

Better still, yoga aids movement through your full range of motion when hitting weights. With a full range of motion, you can build long and full-toned muscles or abs. Physical fitness experts are of the view that stretching yoga poses elongate the protective heath of connective tissues that cover muscles and its cells and repair worn out muscles.

The main reason why yoga energizes and strengthens muscle groups is the long deep breaths, something you have to do as you practice yoga asanas. These deep breaths supply oxygen to the muscles, and boost your ability to focus on workouts.

Yoga can fit into a busy or sedentary lifestyle. Further, some research shows that yoga can heal chronic pain such as migraines. Without much effort, a beginner yogi such as yourself can learn how to make informed health choices and practice specific yoga asanas and techniques aimed at improving your health. This lifestyle coaching can include various aspects like stress reduction, exercising, diet, mindfulness, and other relaxation techniques.

Here Is A Preview Of What You Can Learn From This Book.

- The Basics of Yoga
- Why Practice Yoga?
- How to Adopt Yoga in 4 weeks: A Three Step Approach
- 4-Week Step By Step Guide

Check out the rest of the book by searching for this title on Amazon website.

Preview Of
'Mindfulness for Beginners: 21-Day Step By Step Guide to Relieve Stress and Find Peace in Your Everyday Life'

Introduction

If you have found that life is putting too many strains on you, or that the load that you are left to carry is too heavy, mindfulness may be the answer. People work their minds too hard sometimes. We are taught to think about our actions before we actually put them into practice. We are taught to think before we speak. In today's society, if we had time to relax and enjoy life, it's unlikely that we would, because such are the demands of a modern era. However, when you find out about mindfulness and start to use it, you begin to see things in a very different light. For example, you notice things you didn't notice before. Why? The problem with our philosophy on life is that we tend to look inward instead of seeing what's going on around us.

There are many books on mindfulness and some of them are useful while others seem to be regurgitated information, rather than being of any substance. The difference with this book is that it's written by someone who teaches people to use mindfulness to help improve the quality of their lives. Mindfulness isn't a fad. In fact, it has been taken so seriously by doctors that prescriptions are even being written for students to attend classes to help them to get over the problems associated with stress and anxiety. The success rate is astounding when you compare with traditional treatment using medications. Did you know, for example, that statistics show that in America today, the use of medications for stress related illnesses has increased to a worrying degree but that the figures of people who suffer from anxiety are not going down? Doesn't that tell you something about the efficiency of traditional treatment?

In this book, we look at the possibility of using Mindfulness to be more aware of life, rather than hiding behind medication. Our 21-day step-by-step approach should be sufficient to make you feel less stressed by the end of the 21 days and ready to embrace a fresh approach to anxiety. You won't feel overwhelmed by it. You will feel that you are more in control of your life and you will also feel calmer in demeanor. We would suggest that you follow the steps within the book and try it. You have nothing to lose if you are already stressed to the max and are looking for a solution. Doctors in the United Kingdom have been using Mindfulness to help those suffering with stress because they have recognized that there is little benefit in stifling people with medications that cause patients to be trapped in a vicious cycle. I am depressed – Take anti-depressants – Hide behind the drugs so that you don't have to face the world or the reasons for your unhappiness. Now look at what Mindfulness does. I am depressed though willing to seek out solutions to make my life better, and will use Mindfulness to achieve inner peace and happiness. I know which way you would rather go.

Chapter 1 – Introduction to Mindfulness
Days 1-3

"If you want to conquer the anxiety of life, live in the moment. Live in the breath" ~ Amit Ray

If you are on medication for anxiety related illnesses, it is not suggested that you come off these medications without any kind of medical supervision, but you can start to introduce mindfulness into your life – even when you are taking these medications. The problem with taking medications is that you can't just go "cold turkey" and should not put your body through this kind of treatment. We suggest that you follow the steps shown in this book and when you feel a lot stronger, you can approach your medical professional and adjust your medication, so that you take control of your life.

Day one to three

Step 1 – Learning how your subconscious mind works

Your mind is programmed by the life that you live. All the time, your subconscious mind records all of your responses to stimuli. The subconscious doesn't deal with things such as emotions. If you are afraid of snakes and see one, your mind will know that the right way for you to react is to be afraid. Therapists who deal with anxiety such as this usually suggest introducing stimuli in small controlled doses until your mind is able to feel more comfortable with that particular thing. However, life works that way as well. When you are angry, for example, your subconscious recognizes the thing that made you angry. The next time that thing happens, you will be angry again.

However, you can change the pattern of events because if you show your subconscious mind another reaction to those stimuli, it will relearn your pattern of behavior and will not expect you to get angry given the same circumstances – once your mind is trained. The reason mindfulness is so useful is because it empties out preconceptions. You are told to empty the mind of thought and that's contrary to everything we know about reacting. Your subconscious has much more time to work because it's not crowded out with thoughts – either negative or positive – and is able to help you to see things in a much clearer light.

One of the stumbling blocks that people come across that stops them from being positive is that they don't know how to relax. In this step, we teach you to relax as it forms a very important part of mindfulness. When you meditate, for example, you are mindful of your breathing. The trouble with this advice is that most people don't know how to breathe properly. They assume that air going in and out of the body is sufficient to sustain life, but they don't see it as more than that.

Here Is A Preview Of What You Can Learn From This Book.

- Introduction to Mindfulness Days 1-3
- Being Mindful of your Surroundings – Days 4-6
- Learning to Optimize your Meditative Practice – Days 6-10
- Mindful Acceptance – Days 11 to 15
- Exercises in Humility – Days 16 to 18

Check out the rest of the book by searching for this title on Amazon website.

Check Out My Other Books

Below you'll find my other books that are popular on Amazon and Kindle as well.

Chakras For Beginners: The 7 Chakras Guide On How to Balance your Energy Body through Chakra Healing

Yoga: 4-Week Step By Step Guide for Yoga Beginners

Buddhism for Beginners: 8 Step Guide to Finding Peace and Enlightenment in Your Life

Ultimate Self-Mastery Bundle for Beginners 3 in 1 Bundle

Mindfulness for Beginners: 21-Day Step By Step Guide to Relieve Stress and Find Peace in Your Everyday Life

Happiness: A Little Guide To Self-Love And Positive Thinking

Zen for Beginners: 365 Quotes to Guide Your Life to Happiness and Inner Peace

Self-Discipline: 21 Days to Develop Your Confidence, Willpower and Motivation

Habits: 30 Habits in 30 Days that will Change your Life